How to Really Ruin Your Financial Life and Portfolio

How to Really Ruin Your Financial Life and Portfolio

Ben Stein

WILEY

John Wiley & Sons, Inc.

Published by John Wiley & Sons, Inc., Hoboken, New Jersey.
Published simultaneously in Canada.

For general information on our other products and services, or technical support, please contact our Customer Care Department within the United States at (800) 762–2974, outside the United States at (317) 572–3993 or fax (317) 572–4002.

Wiley also publishes its books in a variety of electronic formats. Some content that appears in print may not be available in electronic books. For more information about Wiley products, visit our website at www.wiley.com.

Library of Congress Cataloging-in-Publication Data:

Stein, Benjamin, 1944- author.
  How to really ruin your financial life and portfolio / Ben Stein.
    pages cm
    ISBN 978–1–118–33873–5 (cloth); ISBN 978–1–118–46148–8 (ebk);
    ISBN 978–1–118–46145–7 (ebk); ISBN 978–1–118–46146–4 (ebk)
    1. Portfolio management.   2.   Investments.   3. Finance,
  Personal.   I. Title.
  HG4529.5.S717 2012
  332.024—dc23

                                                        2012020166

Printed in the United States of America

10 9 8 7 6 5 4 3 2 1

FOR BIG WIFEY+

Contents

Contents

CONTENTS

Contents

CONTENTS

Acknowledgments

The first person I knew who was interested in investing was my mother. She had little training in it, but read *Barron's*, *The Wall Street Journal*, and *Forbes* voraciously. When she died, she left my sister and me a pretty darned good portfolio. She also left me with two fine admonitions: "Buy on the rumor and sell on the news," and, "Bulls make money and bears make money, but hogs get slaughtered." I am not quite sure what either of these mean in practical terms to the long-term, index-oriented investor, but they must mean something because my mother did leave a good portfolio.

My father, a famous economist, was the least interested in money of any man I have ever met, yet he had some excellent wisdom about money. Almost all of it could have been summed up under the simple heading: "Be prudent." I rarely have been since he died in 1999, to my great cost.

My sister, far and away the most prudent Stein now living, and her equally prudent husband, Melvin, have often advised prudence upon me and I thank her and him. My first genius investor mentor was my first agent in Hollywood, George Diskant. His predictions about the economy were not always borne out, but he told me about BRK and that was worth plenty.

Other great influences were my spectacularly good money and banking teacher at Columbia, C. Lowell Harriss, and my superb econ teachers at Yale, Henry Wallich and James Tobin, inventor of "the Fed model" and "Tobin's Q", both designed to tell when the stock market is overvalued and when it is undervalued. Neither seems to have had much predictive value in recent years, but they are certainly correct in general direction.

It has been my great pleasure in the last 25 years to have had a great broker at Merrill Lynch in Kevin Hanley, and more lately in his brilliant colleague, Jerry Au. I have also been privileged to get a general introduction to the erudition of John Bogle. I keep a lot of my stash at Fidelity. I have also made the acquaintance of Ned Johnson and his lovely daughter, Abigail. The Johnsons and their company have done me much good. The Johnsons and John Bogle truly are the small investor's best friends.

For about the last 10 years, I have been a pal and frequent dinner and speaking companion of Ray Lucia, a stunningly well-informed and articulate investment advisor (now retired). I have learned a huge amount from Ray and his brother Joe, whom I consider my own brothers.

If there is anyone smarter in speculation that Jim Rogers, and quicker to see what's happening, I don't know who that would be (unless it's Warren Buffett.) I was on a show with him on Fox for many years and always learned from him and still do. The whole gang on that show, especially host Neil Cavuto, always challenge and impress me.

By an extraordinary twist of fate, I have become pals in the last several years with Warren E. Buffett, surely the greatest genius in investing and in life generally. He is light years ahead of where I will ever be, but he has inspired me and years of reading his annual reports have sparked some kindling in my woolly brain.

Finally, my closest friend, Phil DeMuth, has spent countless hours doing research on investing, often on vague lines I have suggested to him, but usually on his own thoughts. We talk of little else but investing, and it is always useful. Few men that I know have as good a friend as Phil and I am grateful.

Well, maybe that wasn't final. . . . The real acknowledgment is to life its own self. Life has flattened me so many times, lifted me up and laid me down low, given me a wildly false sense of security, then showed me who was boss, taught me so much fear and humility that I felt compelled to offer the lessons in this little book to those younger than I am. "Experience keeps a dear [meaning 'expensive'] school," said Ben Franklin, "but a fool will learn in no other."

I am that fool—but like many a fool at a King's Court, I have seen plenty and can share it. Maybe it can all be summed up by what my Pop said: "Be prudent." But what is prudent? Maybe some idea of it can be gleaned from this book.

Introduction

Your basic human is not a great investor. Successful investing requires extreme patience; we humans are impatient. Rewarding investing requires nerves of steel—or else perfect forgetfulness; we humans are frightened, nervous animals. Making money by investing requires singleness of purpose; we humans are scattered and distracted, pulled in all directions at once. The great investors carefully think through their moves, guided by eons of experience; we real-life human being investors are rash, impulsive gamblers.

Great investors are not swayed by fads and fancies. The ones with two feet and receding hair are wills-o'-the-wisp, blown all about by what is happening at the moment.

The ones who make money over their lifetimes are steadfast of purpose, well informed, listen to wise guidance, reject counsels of impatience and despair. The real-life investor gobbles up misinformation, listens to fools and knaves, and gyrates wildly in his actions, almost always against his own best interest.

I know all of this. I have seen it in my own life on many an occasion. I have seen it in the lives of men and women I know, even supersmart men and women. They make extraordinary mistakes that cost them real money.

Educations are imperiled. Retirements are jeopardized or lost. All of that comes from making poor investment decisions.

Investors do not do the wrong thing because they want to lose money. They do the wrong thing because they are, well, human. And humans are simply constructed of fear and greed and confusion, while great investors are made up of sterner stuff.

Investing involves making money, or trying to do so. There are billions, trillions of words out there written about how to invest wisely. There are far more than I know about. Among those I do know about, I highly recommend anything by my pal Phil DeMuth, or by Warren Buffett, or by John Bogle, the founder of Vanguard, the world standard in low-cost index investing, a simply great way to invest. *John Bogle on Investing* is as good a book as there is on the subject. If you had to read only one book, this would probably be your choice.

There are so many hopelessly confused books about investing out there it would be impossible to know where to begin listing them, and why bother?

Unfortunately, investing also involves people throwing around their money and putting it in a place where other people can take it away from them. This is a bit like the comment often credited to P. T. Barnum: "There's a sucker born every minute—and two to take him."

Very unfortunately, those two are often lawyers, but even more often, they are in the world of investments. The variety of ways and means by which people can relieve other people of their money is breathtakingly infinite. Newsletters. Conferences. Software. Expensive kinds of investment guidance, sometimes called hedge funds, other times called other names.

Often these schemes are run by men who genuinely want to help the investor and truly do. It is far from true that everyone who handles your money is a thief, and I have the great pleasure of working frequently with men and women who do a great job protecting their clients.

But there are more than enough people out there who, through all kinds of motives, but mostly out of all-too-human self-interest, will not have much hesitation in deciding between their interest and yours.

My late father, Herbert Stein, an extremely smart man and a world famous economist, devised what he called Milken's Law, which, he believed, often explained investment options presented to the public by promoters. It went as follows: The constant ME is always greater than the variable U.

It is sad but it's true.

Over the last many years, your humble servant, *moi*, has written and published many books seeking to help investors make sound decisions. I have given so many speeches about it that it scares me. I always preach the basics. But listeners often do not care to hear the basics. They want frills and fads and they usually are wrong to point themselves in that direction. Men and women make terrible mistakes, often because someone they trusted told them to do so.

So I guess making affirmative suggestions to investors has not worked very well, or at least not perfectly.

Now I am going to try a slightly different approach. I am going to suggest ways to ruin your investment portfolio. That's right: I am suggesting ways to ruin your portfolio. Possibly, if you see that you are doing some of these things, you will step back and think about whether you really want to make such efforts at self-destruction. Or maybe you won't. I know that I rarely learn from experience until I have been hit over the head a million times. Maybe the approach of this book will be more helpful than that.

Long ago, when I was a speechwriter for Mr. Richard Nixon and observed his speeches, I learned a great lesson: When a speaker starts a speech, the main thing the audience wants is for him to finish.

Possibly the same is true for books about how to ruin your portfolio, so let me start right away so you can finish right away.

Chapter 1

Trade Frequently

You've been in a casino. You've watched hockey. You've watched tennis. You know it's all about "the action." It's about rapid, speedy moves, about drama, about sudden changes. That's why it's exciting.

Investing in a broad index fund and just letting it sit there, as John Bogle and Warren Buffett and Ben Stein and Phil DeMuth advise, is boring. It is slow. It is like watching paint dry. Why do it? What if the historical data shows you almost always do better by just buying the index and holding it rather than by frequent trading? What if those data are overwhelming and go back over many decades? What if they conclusively prove that jumping in and out of the market leads to returns so much lower than buying and holding—that you might as well just keep the money under your pillow as trade frequently? What if they show that this is true not only for 80 years in the United States but all over the world where stock corporations are allowed? So what?

Those data were about average returns from average investors. You don't want average returns. You are not an average John Q. Investor. You are Superman or Superwoman. You want super returns and you are going to get them. And again, by definition, if you just buy and hold broad swaths of the market, you get the returns of the total market over long periods. Guess what: That's not good enough for you. Not even close.

Instead, you go, guys and gals, go for frequent trading.

There are many ways to approach this. Here is one obvious winner: Buy some new proprietary trading software, load it into the old Mac, turn on the computer, and let'er rip!

The people who made that software knew what they were doing. They aren't just scamming you. They are unbelievably rich billionaires. And they got that way from trading stocks. Yes, they are keeping it quiet, but they are way beyond Warren Buffett in terms of their success at investing.

They have to be, don't they? Yes, of course they do. How else would they have the stones to tell you how to trade? How else would they have the sheer genius to develop and market a brilliant system to trade a lot and beat the market? They are geniuses. I just told you a million times now.

But they are not like those mean-spirited, harmful, stingy billionaires President Obama talks about. They are kind-hearted, generous, super billionaires. They want to share their secrets with you so you'll be part of The Billionaires Club, too.

They aren't selling this software to make a piddling few bucks on each disc they sell or every program you download. That would be beneath them. Those are pennies to men and women like them. They have billions, maybe trillions, from their investing acumen and their trading brilliance. So they don't sell this software to make money.

No, they sell this stuff for one reason and one reason only. They want you to be rich. That's their sincere motivation.

And how do you get to be rich? Rapid, lightning-fast trading.

After all, hasn't everyone who bought those programs and acted on them gotten to be rich?

So, listen to late-night infomercials. Watch them and pay attention. Order the software, and then go out and get rich.

Or, maybe you don't need software. Maybe you just need to watch CNBC starting very early in the morning, and then to trade on the rich golden nuggets they produce for you day after day, hour by hour, minute by minute. The people on those shows have the most up-to-date inside information. They can get you the 411 before the high-frequency traders or the hedge fund boys and girls get it.

They are brimming over with tips and gossip that if acted upon speedily will make you rich.

CNBC is free in most parts of America. It is like owning an oil well or a huge natural gas shale deposit. Just watch it, pay attention to it, and trade like the dickens.

For example, if you see that a corporation is about to issue good earnings news, or has just issued good earnings news, buy that sucker and right now!

Well, wait a minute. There is an old saying that goes, "Buy on the rumor. Sell on the news." So maybe you should sell on the news of good earnings. It varies case by case. But in any event, do SOMETHING right away.

Likewise, if a company has missed its earnings targets, you have to act on that, too. Now, there is one little problem: Sometimes companies that have just missed their earnings projections go down a lot and sometimes they go up a lot. This, however, is no problem for you, the devout CNBC watcher. You just watch and listen to see what the market is doing about the stock in question, and then you do the opposite. Or maybe it's that you do the same.

But no matter. You just do something right away. Maybe just go where the rest of the market is going. Or maybe go against. It is a bit confusing, but for heaven's sake, do something.

Then, of course, there are columns and columnists in magazines and newspapers. They often have tidbits about where certain stocks are going. Pay attention.

These guys and gals are SMART. They didn't get their little desk out in the middle of a floor in an office building in New York City by being stupid. They know things. They can shoot the eyes out of a fly at 100 yards as far as stock picking goes. Don't worry that they are just being fed gossip about the market by men and women who stand to gain by what they whisper to the newspaper and magazine columnists. Don't worry that the big boys are routinely trading against the very advice they whisper to the newspaper columnists. Just do something.

Likewise, when there is any kind of news in the papers or online, trade. Is there war in Syria? That could mean something about oil prices. Do something!

Is there the rumor of a showdown of Israel versus Iran? Again, don't just pretend you can sit this one out. You can't. You have to be in there trading, trading, trading. No *ifs*, *ands*, or *buts*. Is there a presidential candidate who seems likely to win and has announced a plan for a tax on oil companies? Then sell those suckers right this minute. Or maybe buy them because of that "buy on the rumor, sell on the news" thing. Is there bad weather in Guinea-Bissau in West Africa? They must sell something or make something there. Buy it or sell it. Scour the newspapers minute by minute and then trade frantically on the news. That is how the big boys do it. You want to wear the big-boy pants, don't you?

And keep close track of what CNBC and other reliable sources tell you about how the powerful hedge funds are trading. For example, once again—and I know this caution must be boring to a riverboat gambler like you—don't worry that the billionaires are telling you to buy just as they are selling and telling you to sell just as they are buying. They wouldn't do that. They are on Wall Street. That means their word is their bond.

Like the people who are selling trading software, they are not doing what they do to make money. They do it to help you. What other motivation could they have? Surely it wouldn't be to make money off a good guy or gal like you, right?

The newspaper columnists are sworn to helping you, too. They are not interested in their own careers or what they can do to curry favor with these rich Wall Street guys so there might be a taste of honey for them down the road. No, they want to help you. That is their only motive. They are journalists. They live by their honor.

Plus, don't waste your time worrying that if the advice or the gossip is in that day's *Wall Street Journal* or on CNBC, then about 100 million people have already seen the advice and acted upon it. No, no, no. That advice is still fresh and green and useful. Use it. Act on it. Have fun with it. Make money with it.

Now here, perhaps, is a little secret of investing just for you: You may not need any guidance of any kind— not CNBC, not newspapers and magazines, not trading programs. Your own inner guidance and intuition may be more than enough to get the job done.

Yes. Just by a feeling you get at the end of your fingertips when you see the name of a stock rushing by on a computer screen, you will know whether to buy or sell if you are in tune with what George Lucas aptly called "the force." If the force is with you (and it is), you will know when (and much more vitally WHAT) to buy and sell.

Why, your servant, *moi*, just happened to know a young man who came into an inheritance. He had a computer. He had broadband access. He was soon trading just because he felt like it. The results? Well, he was wiped out and his parents had to get a second mortgage on their home to meet their son's debts. But this will not happen to you! Not a freaking chance in the world. You will make money from day one.

So, don't just sit there and watch the paint dry. Go out and trade, trade, trade.

By the way, here's an unexpected side benefit: Whatever brokerage you are using will love you for it. They will be your pals, and call you and thank you and send full-color advertisements so you can trade more and more often. They might even send you a calendar and a birthday card. They will surely send you a Christmas card.

Trade early and often. That's the way the alpha dogs do it, and you are the alpha dog!

Chapter 2

Trade Foreign Exchange

Possibly you remember from The New Testament about the part where The Carpenter cleared The Temple, that is, He tossed out the money changers who had set up shop in the Holy Temple in Jerusalem? Well, guess what! They're ba–ack. Maybe not in the Temple, but they're back.

Yes, the moneychangers, the people who exchange one form of money for another, are back in spades. (Also in clubs, diamonds, hearts, and no trump.) They are totally ready to welcome you to their elite brotherhood.

And quite a club it is. You may not know this, but the foreign exchange (forex) market is by far the largest market in the world. It runs 24/7 all around the world. Christmas. Easter. Rosh Hoshanah. For those who like to make bets all around the clock and who like to particularly make big bets, it's the best casino game on the planet. There are no sexy Keno girls and no one offering you free drinks to play card games and no free Buffalo wings, but it is an immense worldwide casino.

And it's so exotic. Much more exotic than Las Vegas. It takes place all over the world, man. The whole world.

Faraway places with strange sounding names. Currencies from all over the world. Currencies from China and Japan and Taiwan and Russia and Argentina and the Eurozone and even from our own North America.

They are all trading against each other around the clock. Just going, going, going. Yen. Renminbi. Peso. Dollar. Pound. Euro. Zloty. Forint. It's everywhere. There are over a hundred currencies.

And absolutely no one, and I mean NO ONE, knows where the hell they are going or in what direction or how much or for how many seconds, minutes, hours, or days.

The smartest men and women, with the absolute most training in finance and international economics do not know where the currencies are going.

The value of a currency of a nation depends upon the interest rates of that nation relative to other nations, to the trade surplus or deficit of the nation, to the economic health of the nation, to rumors and truths about minerals in that nation. There are political and military causes that move the currencies. There are health scares that move money.

It gets a lot more complex than that. Because you are always buying or selling one currency with another currency, and often involving several more variables than that. All of them are fluctuating every instant of every day, like the blood pressure of a parent with an insolent and lazy child. It is like picking one ant out of a million ants and trying to bet on how long that ant will live and exactly where on the ant heap he will be in a given number of seconds or hours or days. No, it's like picking out one grain of sand and trying to predict where, in a sandstorm, exactly, to within an inch, that grain of sand will wind up.

That tells you that even the smartest, most well-trained minds can often be far off when telling you where currency prices are going. And that, in turn, tells you that no one, as I said above (and I mean NO ONE), knows where a currency will be a day from now or a week from now or ever. The highest ranked math PhD from M.I.T. has about as much chance of getting it right as he does of guessing the weather a month from now.

Immense investment banks like Goldman Sachs and Morgan Stanley have the highest paid, smartest, most well-educated men and women on the planet working for them, many of them trading forex. They are in New York, Paris, London, Hong Kong, Tokyo. They have computers with speed and power beyond reckoning. They can generate scenarios and likelihoods the way you and I smear butter on toast. They can play with more or less unlimited funds.

They collect inside information. They have webs of people who are fantastically well connected all over the planet telling them the latest info on how affairs are going country by country. They have everything that money and property and prestige can buy to make money on foreign exchange.

And they STILL manage often to lose money. Sometimes a single trader can lose billions all by himself. Those rogue traders can be in New York or Tokyo or Paris. They get in the news, sometimes on the front page. But Goldman Sachs and Morgan Stanley and all of the others keep coming back to speculate in forex.

Surely this tells you something. It tells you that how these trades turn out is largely a matter of fate or kismet, if you will. But—and this is a huge BUT—this means it could easily be you who figures out where the yen goes versus the renminbi or the pound or the zloty. If no one can figure it out, if even the best and the brightest at Goldman Sachs cannot figure it out, then (maybe) it's just like buying a lottery ticket. It's not art and it's not science (maybe). It's luck. And, speaking of luck, haven't you often bought lottery tickets? And haven't you occasionally won, even if only a few dollars?

And deep down in your heart, don't you consider yourself a lucky man or woman?

That means you might as well sit in your attic night after night looking at a computer/Internet screen and try to figure it all out. And, once you do figure it out, you can pounce.

You can set up trades that involve many different currencies at once. You can set up trades that involve shorting one currency, or betting it will go down while you go long on other currencies and bet they will go up. There will be trades where you can even go on margin and borrow to make your profits. You can set up a long string of trades where if everything goes right, you can make a jillion dollars. You can make trades that involve currencies, bonds, stock, commodities, options, you name it, and there will be someone there to take your bet. The whole world is one huge bookie joint today, and that goes double where foreign exchange is concerned.

Yes, I know what you are asking. "Are there perhaps software programs that will allow me to just let the computer and its brains, the software, do the hard part without my having to figure it all out? After all, I have to watch the football games." Why, yes, indeedy. There are plenty of these. Available by the bushel. You can even buy more than one and see if their suggestions, all made possible by online streaming of the very most up-to-date data for everything the human mind can contemplate, go for the same smart trade. If that happens, it's like shooting fish in a barrel. Like shooting fish in a barrel after the water has drained out and the fish have stopped flopping, to use a Buffett analogy.

So, yes, yes, yes. Trade forex and make trades in forex a big part of your portfolio.

Chapter 3

Believe in Your Heart That You Can Pick Stocks

Do you sincerely want to be rich? That was a question that Bernie Kornfeld, a latterly convicted swindler, used to ask his audiences as he pitched them on the merits of buying his product, a "fund of funds" that used investors' money to buy several layers of mutual funds. At most or all of the stages, Mr. Kornfeld charged steep fees to the investors when those same investors could have just bought the funds themselves for modest fees. (Of course, those fees were chump change compared with what hedge fund managers now charge, but that's another story.) Mr. Kornfeld himself did sincerely want to be rich. He used his winnings to buy lavish homes and beautiful women—or at least so he considered them. Eventually, he went to prison for fraud in faraway Switzerland.

But that is a digression. His basic question still makes a lot of sense. Do you sincerely want to be rich?

If you do—and who doesn't—then you must step up to the plate and swing for the fences. That means you have to try to pick the stocks that will outperform the market. You do not want to just buy the broad indexes like the Dow Diamonds, an index that replicates generally the performance of the Dow Jones 30 industrial stocks. Yes, just buying and holding this index over the postwar period would have given you returns vastly superior to those of almost any managed mutual fund or portfolio of wealth managers. The data is overwhelming on that point.

There is simply no way that even the most well-trained, most intelligent investment managers have been able to beat the Dow over long periods except in the rarest of cases.

But that means that your investments would be merely keeping up with the market. Your investments would be performing at best in an average way. You are not an average guy. So why should you shoot to be average in your investment returns?

Never mind that just keeping up with the average of the Dow will give you returns stupendously superior to the returns of almost every stock picker over long periods. Your friends at the golf course will still consider your returns "average," and what is there to brag about in that?

Likewise, you don't want to buy the Spiders, the index that closely (not exactly) replicates the returns of the Standard & Poor's 500 Stock Market Index— generally speaking, the stocks of the 500 largest publicly traded corporations in America.

Yes, true, data has been amassed showing that while there will be years in which many stock pickers outperform the S&P 500 Index, over long periods almost no one outperforms buying and holding that index. Yes, just recently in the chaos and terror following the banking and real estate crisis of 2008, there were a goodly number of money managers whose funds out-performed the Spiders. That was because the Spiders were heavily weighted toward banking and financial stocks and those were deeply wounded in the Crash of 2008 while nimble money managers might have been able to get out of that sector before the worst damage was done.

Nevertheless, over long periods, even over the period following the crash until now, as I am writing in spring 2012, the S&P 500 has greatly outperformed the huge majority of mutual funds as well as most hedge funds that report results.

Still, that incredibly powerful record of the large indexes beating the stock pickers will not save you from the accusation that you are no better than an average investor. Again, you are doing neither more nor less than settling for average performance.

Of course, "average performance" might be better defined as the average results of average investors, rather than the average returns of the whole market. By that measure, the performance of the indexes beats the achievements of investors by a truly staggering margin.

A genius professor at Emory University named Ilia Dichev and several other geniuses have documented the long-standing truth that rapid trading by the ordinary investor of individual stocks does not yield returns even close to those of buying and holding the broad indexes. The differences are so large as to make stock market investing by picking stocks barely worthwhile. They are so large as to make even being in the stock market at all seem questionable if you are going to jump all around all over the place.

In fact, as your humble scribe writes this, the true super genius of investing, Warren Buffett, is out with his annual Berkshire Hathaway (BRK) report. In it, his letter reaffirms what he has been saying for decades: that even a genius like Buffett cannot outperform the market for long. Indeed, his long-term results for picking stocks, which were once staggering, now barely exceed the S&P 500s performance since the founding of BRK. This, by itself, is hair-raising news. It should make every stock picker unable to sleep at night.

Still, the schoolyard bullies and teases will tell you that you are a chicken and a wimp, and that you are—again—settling for no better than average returns.

You could go for an even wider index—an index that includes virtually every stock of any size at all in the United States, such as the Russell or Wilshire indexes. They would reach into the corners of investing and make your performance even better. Your performance (in particular if you buy and hold) versus the performance of the average stock-picking, trading investor would be spectacularly superior. The differences would be breathtakingly in your favor if you bought and held the widest possible index for all of your working life.

There are even indexes for the whole world. There is, just for example, the Vanguard Total Stock Market Index (VTI), which includes almost every public corporation of any size anywhere in the world. You can buy that and get pieces of the action everywhere, from Switzerland to South Africa to Spain to Sweden, and from the United States to Uruguay and Ukraine, and from Great Britain to Israel. This index would be subject to effects from regional crises such as the current Eurozone problems, but over time, if history is any guide, your results would put to shame the results of men and women who were ordinary or even very good investors.

But, *une fois de plus*, the kids who like to make you cry out by the monkey bars would tell you that your returns were merely average.

The horrible truth is that these bad boys have some truth on their side. Yes, the returns from indexes will be excellent compared with the returns of the average investor. But you will not get the returns that (used to) make a Warren Buffett or a Seth Klarman, genius manager of the hedge fund called Baupost Group. You will get good enough returns to satisfy a normal human being, but that just brings us back to the basic issue:

You are not a normal, average Jane or Joe and you do not want average returns. In your heart, as you very well know, you are legions ahead of those average investors, and even legions ahead of the indexes. You are a superior man or woman, and you must have deeply superior results. You do not want stocks that do well. You want the next super-stock, the next Microsoft, the next Google, the next Facebook. You want the stocks that will go up 10,000 times in value and make you the owner of an estate in Bel Air with showgirls on your arm and doormen bowing and scraping as you walk into the lobby of every fine hotel in the world.

25

That means you have to go past the indexes—way, way past them. You have to roll your sleeves up and do the basic research, the in-depth analysis, the burning of the midnight oil that will get you to the Gates of Eden.

Now, some of those same spoilsports who told you that your results with indexes were merely average will tell you that there are already tens of thousands of young brilliant minds working with every tool in the book to find these great companies. (A mind is a terrible thing to waste.) And with all of the tools and devices on this earth, they rarely if ever beat the markets by picking individual stocks.

These same mean-spirited creeps will tell you that those people (or ones like them) brought us the cata-strophic Internet crash of 2000−2001 and the financial wipeout of 2008−2009. The masters of Wall Street turn out to be outgunned by reality decade after decade. (What is an index-fund investor? A stock picker mug-ged by reality.)

By the way, some might say that those same types of geniuses work for the big mutual funds and bank trust departments, and whose results do not even come close to the results of the indexes. Those same people write the advice-to-the-investment-lorn columns and pick stocks on TV shows that rarely do well over long periods. (How do you know when to sell? When they say to buy.) Those meanies will tell you that, really, there are hardly any ways to beat the market. (These are the nice meanies, not the evil meanies who urged you to get way-above-average returns.)

DON'T LISTEN TO THEM! YOU CAN PICK STOCKS AND BEAT THE MARKET!!!

You don't need libraries and mainframes. All you need is love of yourself, the trust you have in your own fingertips running down the lists of stocks online, and a feeling that tells you when to buy and when to sell.

It's that feeling, not intellectual rigor, not experience—just that feeling—that will take you to the next Facebook, the next Berkshire Hathaway, the next Microsoft. You can pick stocks.

Chapter 4

Assume That Recent Trends Will Continue Indefinitely

A re Internet stocks hot, or were they in 1999? That's great. If they are hot, they'll stay hot. Ooops. They didn't? Well, they'll come back. You say most are in the afterlife? Well, that's an exception. Usually stocks that are hot stay hot.

Are social media stocks hot as I am writing this? They will stay hot. Yes, you can take it to the bank.

Buy as much social media as you can and you will never regret it. There is Newton's first law of motion that says that a body in motion tends to stay in motion. Translated to stocks, that means a sector that's hot will stay hot.

Now, to be sure, there are laws of thermodynamics stating categorically that when an object deviates from the mean temperature in the nearby environment, it will tend to revert to that mean temperature. That is, even hot items will cool down to the general level in the neighborhood.

But that law does not apply to investing. Instead, you want to keep piling into stocks and funds that are hot. They will stay hot. Our friend, Professor Dichev, and many others in his field, have clearly demonstrated with facts and history that when a stock or a sector, or the market generally, is hot (Dichev is more about the market generally), it will cool down. Sometimes it will downright freeze.

So, when money flows into stocks are the largest, and when the market capitalization of stocks generally has risen to abnormal levels—that's when it will soon come down. The prime example might be the Nifty

Fifty of the 1960s. These were superhot stocks like Xerox, Kodak, and Litton that just could do no wrong—they were the wave of the future and you could never lose if you were invested in them. They then turned down and have stayed down for a long time. Too bad for Xerox. They invented Windows but saw little commercial application for it so they gave it away, basically, to a fellow named Gates (and no one's ever heard of him again!). Too bad for Kodak, who did not see digital cameras coming and also did not see Fuji coming. IBM has done well, but the others have been a mixed bag.

Too bad for the Nifty Fifty companies: Most of them learned the hard way about "reversion to the mean." Oh, didn't they tell you about the term "reversion to the mean" back in finance classes, or maybe in statistics? It is the simple rule that if a stock or anything else in the world of randomness—and stocks do live in that world—deviates far from the average (i.e., the mean), it will eventually return to the mean, as the mean is calculated over long periods.

But that does not apply to you. You live in your own special universe. The normal laws of financial entropy (or anything else random and normal) do not apply to you. So, go ahead anyway, and bet the farm on the stocks that are hot right now. You will never be disappointed.

That goes for the stock market as a whole. If it's hot, thanks to the innovations of exchange-traded funds (ETFs) and index funds, you can just buy the whole market. That's what the nerdy kids are doing right now anyway. As I already told you, that's a silly way to go when a genius like you can pick stocks that will out-perform the market. But if you persist in buying indexes, just know that the best time to buy them is when the whole market is sizzling. If it is hot today, it will stay hot.

To be sure, two astonishing geniuses named John Bogle and Warren Buffett, and also Phil DeMuth, another astounding genius, and even pitiful old Ben Stein, have pointed out that when stocks rise a lot, usually it's somewhat because of rising earnings—which is a great thing—and somewhat because Mr. Market is applying a higher valuation to those earnings.

That is, stocks trade as a multiple of their earnings. It's nice when earnings rise, but when the world at large has determined that good times are here for good, and raises the multiple it applies to earnings—that's when things get really great and jiggy. For example, if grouchy old fools think that there should be some caution applied to stocks or maybe to the whole economy, they will say that a stock is worth, say, eight times earnings. That was the way it was long ago in the bad old days of inflation in the 1970s and early 1980s. After all, cranky people argued, if you can get 10 percent on a safe Treasury bond—that was in the days long, long ago when Treasury bonds were considered a safe asset—why should you pay more than eight times earnings for a stock that has uncertainty in it? The stock will be yielding 12.5 percent and the bond will be yielding 10 percent. That seemed about right to those old fuddy duddies. But when "morning came to America" in the Reagan, Bush, and Clinton years, horizons were unlimited. No inflation. Rising earnings. Why shouldn't stocks sell for 30 times earnings? After all, their earnings will soon rise to the point where the stock you bought when it was earnings 3.3 percent will be earning 10 percent. Why not put that in the price right away? Why not hold a stampede to buy? That's when the world suddenly decides that the market is not worth 1,000 on the Dow. Now, it's worth 6,000!

That's when they are using champagne to wash their Bentleys on Wall Street. That's when money is bubbling forth under every sidewalk in Manhattan and Greenwich.

You can be sure that when those days come, they will last. They always do. So, to make sure you fully understand, buy in when things are hot, and keep on buying, buying, buying. They won't go down.

Chapter 5

Pour Continuer . . . Sell When Things Look Bleak . . . and Stay the Heck Out of the Market

That's right. Just as it was vital to buy when things were hot, it's just as vital to sell when they are cool. If stocks take a really big dive, then it's time to sell them, and fast. There is no bottom, really, except for zero, and you sure don't want to be there when the stock market hits zero.

Plus, your friends who say they have already sold will be telling you to sell, and you want to take their fine advice. It's interesting, by the way, that as I navigate through my older years, I can recall with such vividness the friends who comforted me when I was in distress about the stock market by telling me they had sold at the peak. These are good friends indeed, and you can be sure they wish you well. My old Mom used to tell me that her friends would always tell her when they had sold at exactly the right moment but never when they didn't sell at the right moment. And they would discuss the stocks that went right but never the stocks that went wrong. She must have been right. Obviously, not everyone makes all of the right moves in stocks or everyone would be a billionaire and no one would ever lose money. We know that neither of those scenarios is true.

But to get to the main point, it is crucial to realize that when things are looking bad financially and economically and perhaps even politically, there simply is no limit except annihilation to what can happen to your stocks.

Think of Custer at The Little Big Horn. His unit was annihilated by the marauding Native Americans in about a half hour. Can you be sure the same won't happen to you? No, you cannot.

That means it's time to sell when things are looking bleak.

My dear pal Phil DeMuth and I have written a book you can still get called *Yes, You Can Time the Market*. It documents that ordinary investors panic and sell at exactly the wrong time. They suffer from what social scientists call the recency bias. They firmly believe that whatever trend has happened recently will keep on happening. This is the same bias that makes investors buy when the market is rising to what later turns out to be unsustainable levels.

Phil and I documented—as others have as well— that when the market is low in terms of the ratio of price to earnings, when it is low compared with its price history over the past decades, that is when it's generally time to buy, not to sell.

But (and we will get to more on this later), this time it's different. This time, there really and truly is no bottom at all. In fact, this time you might well find that for the first time in history—and even though it's arithmetically not possible—stocks fall to a negative level. That's right. You might well find that you owe money on your portfolio.

So, get out when things are bleak and get out fast. Hoard your cash. You will well know when it's time to get back in. (More about that to come as well.)

When you get out, stay out until you get that certain mysterious golden feeling. You may have heard that if you are out of the market when certain big things happen—like when the market stages a huge turnaround day after day as it did in early March of 2009, you will miss a great chunk of the gains for the whole decade.

You may have heard that there will be a few incredible days when the market is up 3 or 4 percent or even more, and if you miss one of those days, you miss out on an immense share of the market's total gains for your lifetime. You may have heard that the market's total gains over many decades are far from evenly distributed but instead are concentrated on a few explosive days.

But don't worry about that. When you are completely out of the market and one of those spec-tacular days comes along, or rather is about to come along, you will know it by an itching in your fingertips. You'll know when your love comes along, as the old song goes. You will know, and the day before you will buy in at just the right moment to "catch a wave" and be sitting on top of the world.

In fact, that Beach Boys' song captures exactly when it's going to happen to you in your whole life of investing if you just follow the rules in this tome: The world of investing is ruled by certain waves, and if you just trust in yourself, if you really believe in yourself, you can and will do it so you wind up pretty damned rich pretty quick.

So, again, when the market is going down, get out and stay out until the exact moment comes to get right back in. And you'll know it the night before. Or two nights before. Why? Because you are you!

Chapter 6

Know in Your Heart That This Time It's Different . . . and Act on It

Several years ago, I was regularly on a Fox News panel with one of the most successful investor/speculators of all time, a true genius named Jim Rogers. Jim and I were debating about some facet of the stock market and I said something I do not entirely recall.

It was roughly about how even though the Fed was printing so much money, this time it would not create inflation, even though it generally does.

Jim called me on it immediately.

"There you go," he said. "You've just said the most dangerous words in the investors' dictionary: 'It's different this time.'"

Jim is a billionaire many times over, I am sure, and he learned his trade at the school of the redoubtable investor George Soros. Messrs. Soros and Rogers have learned that there are certain recurring themes in investing, and that once you deviate too far from these norms, you are going to get in real trouble. George Soros reportedly made a billion dollars personally, back when that was a lot of money, by selling short the British pound. When the pound was in fact allowed to float radically downward, he reaped the rewards, and he's now free to be a patron to the political causes he endorses. Jim's picks in commodities have proved to be startlingly on target, as he relentlessly applies common sense and arithmetic when the rest of us apply hope and fear.

His point on that panel was brilliant. If you believe that "this time it's different," that this time stocks can

sell at 40 times earnings and stay there, if you believe
that social media companies with no earnings to speak
of are worth as much as GE, if you believe that the
federal government can endlessly go deeper into hock
without someday having a rude awakening—you are
going to be stunned and beaten up badly. That was his
point about the average Joe or Jane.

When pundits and experts say it's going to be different this time, that there is a "new paradigm" or
something like that—look out below. Again, that's for
the average Joe or Janette.

That is what Jim or any other seasoned, successful
speculator would say to most investors. But don't worry
about that: because for you, and only for you, this time
it really will be different.

You can forget all historical precedent and just go
right on with making money and believing there is
a new paradigm. Just for example, this time, the
value of your portfolio will NOT depend on the earnings
of the companies in it. This time, it is possible—
nay, likely—that even if earnings are zero or negative
right now, future earnings will increase so fast that
any historical metric of the price/earnings ratio will

be meaningless and only the new paradigm will make sense.

This time, trees really do grow to the sky. The old verities of investing are, well, OLD. The way you make money is with something NEW. And those are the ideas that earnings don't matter, only growth matters, and that securities are not about generating money but about rising in price based on wild public love of the security.

This brings to mind a painful memory. Back at the end of 1999, as the Internet bubble was frothing madly, and my "old economy" stocks like oil and banks were languishing, I examined the charts for those two kinds of companies. Sure enough, the ones I owned had generated real earnings, sometimes superb earnings. Their prices were pitifully low.

The "new economy" stocks that were soaring off to the moon had no earnings at all, and often had enormous losses.

I thought to myself, "Well, Benjy, what is a security? Isn't it a share in ownership of an entity that generates income (and eventually dividends) for its owners? Doesn't it have to be that?

"Or is it perhaps something else entirely? Perhaps a stock/security is more like a lottery ticket, a wager that the company in which you are buying an ownership stake will someday become the biggest company in the world." That certainly seemed to be the way the market was behaving. That was what the market was telling us.

The shameful part of this memory is that I did not just say to myself, "Why you poor idiotic fool. Of course a security is ownership in something that generates earnings for you. Otherwise it has zero meaning and is not a security but a lottery ticket." Instead, I took some of my life savings and bought some Internet stocks and indexes of Internet stocks.

For several months, the results were staggeringly good. I would sometimes look at the stock prices at the end of the day and actually laugh out loud with glee.

Obviously, that came to a crashing end when the Bubble burst and the stocks I owned that had been trading above 100 times earnings—sometimes priced at over 100 with zero earnings—were suddenly worth at most a few cents. I had asked the right question: Can it possibly be different this time? Can a whole new definition of stocks be the correct definition? But I had given myself the wrong answer. Luckily for me, enough of me was still sane so that I had only taken a small amount out of the sane money world and put it in the insane money world. Still, it hurt like the dickens when it all came crashing down. I had believed that it would be different that time. That was a belief that cost me.

But that won't happen to you! Just because this time it did not turn out to be different for me, that absolutely does not mean it won't be different for you! You and I are not the same person and we each have our own worlds, and in yours things can be different this time. Sometimes, in the world of ownership, earnings simply do not matter.

In Berlin, after the Nazi collapse, the economy was based largely on trading tins of sardines or individual cigarettes. Few Germans had any real money, so they traded the tins and the cigarettes as if they were money. Now, note carefully—they did not eat the sardines. They did not smoke the cigarettes. The sardines and the cigarettes were for trading purposes only, not for the usefulness of the fish or the tobacco in them.

That's how it sometimes is with stocks. Their value grows so fantastically on the exchanges that it's not even remotely connected with how much money they make and sometimes not even with how much revenue they have. Those are days like the days of the Internet Bubble or the Social Media Bubble of right now.

When those days come, get with the program: Buy, buy, buy and don't worry if there is no safety net below the high wire. Don't worry if, to use Warren Buffett's phrase, you're at a masked ball that you have to leave by midnight—only there are no clocks in the room.

You'll do fine anyway because . . . THIS TIME IT'S DIFFERENT!

Chapter 7

Dividends Are for Spending—Not Investing—Just Ignore Them or Use Them to Buy Baubles

There is a smart fellow named Jason Zweig who writes a column about investing for the *Wall Street Journal*. (I recommend him as I recommend the *Journal* altogether, the business section of the *New York Times*, and *Barron*'s, the best there is.) In early March of 2012, Zweig had a column about how high the stock market was as it hovered slightly above and slightly below 13,000 on the Dow.

His very smart points were that the Dow was not at an all-time high, but it was certainly very high. He noted that adjusted for inflation, however, it was far from an all-time high. (Actually, adjusted for inflation, it took the Dow about 60 years to reach its 1929 peak, not counting inflation and dividends. I told you that. Mr. Zweig could have told you that in his sleep, I am sure.)

Mr. Zweig brought in one of the big guns in the statistics of finance, Professor Meir Statman of Santa Clara University, to calculate—among many other calculations—what the Dow would be if you had owned the Dow since it started in roughly 1896 and had reinvested all of the dividends back into the Dow. What would the Dow be? This was a difficult calculation to make because so many of the stocks in the Dow are long dead and buried or moved out of the Dow, but he did it anyhow. I'll have to track him down and find out how he did it.

That's not the point. If you had bought the Dow when it was at about 10 in 1896 and had received and reinvested all of the dividends, and if they had compounded at the same rate as the Dow itself, your own Dow would not be 13,000.

It would be 13 MILLION.

That would seem like a good reason to reinvest your dividends, wouldn't it? To make them grow and to grow rich.

But wait a minute. Life is finite. Life does not go on forever. Life is short. Sometimes we have to party hearty.

Yes, you would have more money in your portfolio now, or at least a greater value of the money, but you would also have had less party time, less beer, fewer big screen HDTVs to watch, and fewer ATVs to flip over. You would have been a dreary Scrooge, a flinty, no-fun accountant type to just keep all those dividends in your account and not spend them.

Now it's my job to be fair. So I have to note that long ago, when the Dow was young, and even up until a couple of decades ago, the dividend payout rate of stocks of some size like the ones in the Dow was far higher than it is now. Even in most of the Great Depression, the Dow paid between 6 and 8 percent in dividends. Even in the space age of the 1960s and 1970s, the Dow commonly paid in the 6 and 8 percent range.

Those high pay outs, compounded over dogs' years, made the Dow worth roughly 1,000 times more, with dividends reinvested from the start of the Dow until now, than without dividends.

Those days are ancient history. Now the Dow pays less than 2 percent in dividends. That's so little that you might as well spend it or else just let it sit in your brokerage account earning 0.1 percent or less. Why even bother to think about it?

Compound interest is a big fat fraud. Don't even think about that either. Just because it can totally and utterly change your life to allow compound interest to work in your portfolio, still, don't think about it at all. Just because one of the greatest economists of all time, Milton Friedman, said that compound interest was the greatest invention of all time, don't pay any attention to your dividends. Just take them out when they appear in your portfolio and spend them.

While we're on the subject, let's talk about, "Why even bother to think about dividends at all?"

The new-age stocks, the ones that really pop, have no dividends at all most of the time. If they do pay a dividend, it's likely to be a pretty pitiful one. So, why pay attention to whether a stock even pays a dividend?

True, some of those same stodgy, belt-and-suspenders guys who talk to you about there being no new paradigm may tell you that dividends matter a lot.

They'll say that if a company consistently pays dividends, it shows the company is consistently earning money. They'll say that if a company consistently earns dividends and is able to raise its dividends, it's probably got a good product or service and is well managed and might occupy a space without Far Eastern competition. The business might actually have enough staying power to last for a few decades in your portfolio.

They might even tell you that such stocks—those with good dividends, when dividends are compounded—tend to greatly outperform stocks that have either no dividends or low dividends.

They'll tell you that this is caused by the effect of compounding plus the fact that if a company can pay real dividends, it's a real company with money coming in at a greater rate than it's going out.

Plus, they will possibly also tell you that high-dividend stocks—and here we mean stocks that consistently pay a good dividend out of earnings, not stocks that have a huge dividend because the price has collapsed and the old dividend before being cut (as it inevitably will be) seems momentarily to be immense, tend to fluctuate less in a negative direction than stocks that have no dividend.

Here, they may be talking to you about so-called low-beta stocks, meaning stocks that fluctuate less than the market in general, and how that low beta is generated by a steady flow of dividends.

The low-beta part might just be because high dividend (high sustained dividend) stocks have an anchor to windward. Their price does not move just on anticipation of the future, either for them or for the markets in general.

No, they are at least partially priced like a bond, meaning that their price is at least in some measure a multiple of the dividend, and that can and will mean that as long as the dividends are paid, their price will be a bit more stable, as bond prices tend to be (but not always) when compared with stocks.

And they may say that high-dividend/low-beta stocks show greater appreciation over long periods than low- or no-dividend stocks.

Don't listen to them. How big a dividend did Microsoft pay for most of its life? How big a dividend does Google pay? How big a dividend will Facebook pay? How long before March 2012 did Apple go without paying a dividend? Something like 18 years. Yet that stock was a money spinner for anyone who held it over a prolonged period.

And most of all, how long has it been since Berkshire Hathaway, that gem of gems until recently, paid a dividend? Answer to the last question: BRK has never paid a dividend. (But your humble scribe thinks they will soon.)

Now, those same skinflint, green eye-shades guys will say, "Well, good luck picking the next one of those, pal. Yes, there will be a few that don't pay a dividend and turn out to be solid gold. But as a general matter, high-dividend stocks pay off far better over time than low-dividend stocks."

Don't listen to them. Stuff cotton in your ears. Those are the same fools who will tell you that you cannot pick stocks in the first place.

Of course you can, and of course you will, pick the low- or no-dividend stocks that will do fantastically well. So, for now and forever, just ignore the stocks that pay good dividends and when a dividend-paying stock lands in your portfolio by some chance, spend those dividends pronto. DO NOT REINVEST THEM! Buy your lover a bracelet or a car. Buy yourself a trip to Jamaica. Life is short. Have a good time with it.

Chapter 8

Cash Is Garbage— Except When It's Not

Have you looked at your bank statements or money market account statements lately? It's mighty discouraging. Basically, you get no interest at all. On some accounts at some banks, you get literally one hundredth of one percent per year to invest with them.

That's cruel. I can recall back in the early 1980s when you could get 12, 13, 14 percent on fairly short-term

CDs. It seems to me that there was a time when some CDs were approaching 15 percent interest. Of course that was when the economy was being choked into submission by Paul Volcker, chairman of the Fed, after a prolonged period of unacceptably high inflation. But never mind. There was a time when interest paid in the teens. It really happened.

So what's this nonsense about basically no interest on your cash? Why bother to have it there at the bank or money market account at all? Your cash ain't nothing but trash at these interest rates.

We all know that there are reasons why these current rates are so low. The Federal Reserve is committed to a Zero Interest Rate Policy to stimulate the economy. They buy Treasury bonds in immense quantities to keep the interest rates super low. You cannot fight the Fed and so you cannot search around and find higher interest rates hidden away in some small town where they haven't heard of the Federal Reserve. These low rates on cash are universal. (Although, life is unpredictable. Even as I am writing this, there are rumblings that the economy is reviving and interest rates might rise by a tiny amount. Stay tuned.)

Ordinary mom-and-pop investors pay the price for these super-low rates. He or she slaves and saves for decades and then gets almost no interest to support him or her in retirement. Again, it is cruel.

Yet, we have inflation. By federal government statistics, we have had between 3 and 4 percent inflation over the last several years. So, if we get .01 percent on our savings, we are actually losing money—and a lot of money at that—if we just leave our money in cash at our local bank or at our national money market fund. (You would think there would be blood in the streets about it, but somehow, there isn't. The American saver is a fairly passive guy or gal.)

But why play along with the Fed's silly game? Why not just forget about cash altogether and plunk it down somewhere in the land of juicy returns? There are plenty of places where that money gets a good return either in capital gains or bond coupons.

The stock market staged a stupendous rally from March 2009 to mid-March 2012, rocketing from roughly 6,500 on the Dow to above 13,000. And that's with the economy still extremely fragile. There are still cracks in the Eurozone. China, the wheel horse for international trade, has been faltering; although to be sure from a super, unbelievably high rate of around 10 percent growth per annum to a merely amazing rate of about 8.5 or 9 percent per annum.

Unemployment is still well above 8 percent in the United States as I write this in spring 2012 (although it is trending down consistently), and the federal fiscal situation is dire indeed. We have staggering deficits and no immediate prospect of cutting them. We have real fears that the government might someday actually default on its debt. (It is actually more than a fear. It is a certainty.)

Here's my point: If, in these parlous times, the stock market has staged such a momentous rally, what is it going to do when the recovery really gets rolling? Will there be any stopping it short of 20,000 on the Dow? Why not 30,000? Why not 35,000?

In that case, why don't you just lay down all of your cash on the stock market? You can pick stocks, since we already know you are really, really good at doing that. Or you can do what the squares do, and buy index funds. But why not plunge into the stock market with both size 13s?

After all, the stock market already had its big correction in 2008–2009. That's already happened.

It couldn't happen again, could it? Not so soon after the first crash. (Or maybe I should say the most recent crash?) There would be no precedent for the stock market collapsing by roughly 60 percent then coming back and then falling a lot again, would there?

Well, actually, yes. There have not just been some, but many times when the stock market rallied like crazy—and then, on some unexpected piece of bad news or even on some widely anticipated piece of bad news—fell like a stone.

All through the early 1970s and 1980s, the market see-sawed. To be sure, the highs always got higher (except when you adjust them for inflation, but that's another dismal story and I don't want to ruin your day). But over periods of years, the markets can fall and rise and fall crazily.

No one can see it coming, and that's the problem and the opportunity. You see, while the market in general cannot see it coming—YOU CAN SEE IT COMING. So, while some of those dismal stodgy types might say that you never can tell when the market will tank and that therefore you should keep some money in cash, don't let that thought enter your mind.

Yes, absolutely true, some cranks might warn you. They might tell you that you could use up all of your cash and buy stocks and it might well turn out that you were buying at the top (at least for a while), and then when the market collapses, it takes you down with it. Whoops. There goes your money.

Those same Cassandras might tell you that you might want to keep some of your money liquid and available so that if the market really falls, you can have some cash to buy in at the new lower levels.

But why listen to them? You will start to get a tingling in your toes when the market is about a month away from crashing. You will start to have dreams of your forgotten ancestors telling you that it's high time to sell out the following morning. You'll know and you can get out of the market, have a wad of cash, and be ready to buy in when the new low approaches.

I know what you're thinking. "How will I know when that new low is on the way or already here?"

Some will tell you that you cannot know. That even the most savvy traders do not know. Some will tell you that you cannot possibly know even by the use of forecasting models used by the most powerful investment banks and hedge funds.

The behavior of markets is simply too confusing and difficult to predict for you or anyone on Wall Street or in Greenwich, Connecticut, to be able to figure out what that bottom is or what to do about it. After all, look in your newspapers and magazines. Look it up on line. How many men and women called the bottom in the beginning of March 2009?

(Actually, I do know of one: Doug Kass, a very smart fellow out of Florida. He runs some money and he's a damned smart guy. But I don't know of any others who called that bottom. Dougie is one of many thousands of money managers, and he would be the first to admit that he's been wrong on other occasions.)

But again, YOU will know what to do. You will see how you can beat the market over and over again, and you'll do it. You will use up all of your cash to buy stock tomorrow. You will ride the market up to its high. Then you'll sell and raise cash. Then you'll buy in again at exactly the right moment. That's you, pal. Count on it. It's a sure thing.

Or, if you want really high current income, you can try for junk bonds.

What is a junk bond, you may ask? First of all, it's not really junk. It's only called a junk bond. It is really a perfectly fine bond that pays interest at a much higher rate than other bonds or CDs or savings accounts.

Even now, when CDs pay essentially zilch and high-grade bonds pay 4 or 5 percent, junk bonds pay 6, 7, and 8 percent. And yet they are bonds. That means they are a sacred obligation to pay by the entity that issued them. That means a promise in blood.

The jealous, envious issuers like GE or Ford might call the bonds of another company junk. But that's because they are jealous of how much of a coupon the junk pays.

Really, a junk issuer might be a start-up with no established credit. It might be an older company temporarily down on its luck. It might be an older company that has been taken over by a private-equity company that has bought it, and then issued a ton of bonds against it to pay back its own investors a tad early for the trouble they have gone to so as to reinvigorate the company.

But the point is that these bonds can pay a ton of interest in the form of much higher yearly or quarterly coupons than anything else around yields. And isn't high current interest what you're looking for?

So, make it easy on yourself. Buy into junk bonds in a big, big way. You can pick them individually or you can buy a junk bond fund (a mutual fund of junk, painstakingly selected by brilliant bond analysts). Or you can buy a junk exchange-traded fund, which is a lot like a mutual fund of junk only it trades all through the day instead of once a day like a mutual fund. In any of them, you will get much higher interest rate than on cash or highly rated bonds.

Now, some may say that junk bonds have that name because they are risky and sometimes simply collapse and stop paying their coupons, and then you are out of luck.

So, what? Life itself is risky, brother. You could get hit by a truck. Isn't it worth taking that risk to get super-high interest?

Of course it is.

Some may tell you that there have been times, such as upon the collapse of the super, uber-junk issuer Drexel

Burnham Lambert, where virtually all of the bonds issued by that venerable firm vaporized. Only the underwriters, led by the redoubtable Michael R. Milken, made out well. (He went to prison, actually, but handled it enviably bravely, and he is still a multibillionaire, a philanthropist, and a host of economic conferences.) The bondholders got creamed and their vaunted interest-rate advantage was gone.

Indeed, some creeps will tell you that junk is often a sign of issuers who do not really and truly plan to repay the loans. One of the most famous issuers, a man I happen to know, a clever fellow named Meshulam Riklis, supposedly once told his colleagues that he would never repay a junk bond. He would always replace it with a new bond or he would default. He became a fabulously rich man, surrounded by beautiful women such as Pia Zadora.

There is some considerable data that shows that over long periods—except when the United States was leaving the Great Depression to begin the phenomenal prosperity of the Second World War—junk underperformed high-grade issuers because the junk default rate was so high.

Your humble author spent a huge period of his life studying all of this and writing about it for *Barron's*. My basic conclusion: I would not want my son to be invested in junk.

It seemed to me like a come-on and a Ponzi scheme in some instances.

But that's just me. I am an old fool. Disregard what I say and go for the high rates on junk. No one will swindle you. You are far, far too clever for that.

Nor need you worry that a credit crunch that shakes highly rated debt, as did the one in 2008—2009, will simply vaporize junk as has happened in the past. If there is a major default in the Eurozone that rattles windows as far as Arkansas, it may make everyone else's bonds fall drastically—but not yours.

You do not need to worry that there are men and women who spend their whole lives studying junk bonds. Yes, true—they do come up with some amazing finds that eventually make a great deal of money on some of that junk. Even the U.S. Treasury, who often cannot find their backsides with both hands, bought an immense amount of poorly rated bonds and other credit instruments during the Crash of 2008—2009—

and sold them in 2011 and 2012 and made at least $25 billion on the trades.

I, who know this field a bit, will tell you that you do not have the staying power of the Treasury Department. And those crafty, well-trained credit analysts who really truly can spot the gems in junk . . . well, they do not work for you. They work for someone else. Someone much closer to them. They won't be working for you. They are not going to tip you off to where to go for those super finds in the world of junk. They work for and with a small crowd of insiders in the world of junk. That's what I would tell you.

Never mind me. I am just a crank. Go for those high-paying junk bonds right now. Leave behind your fears and the facts of history. Those lush yields are money in the bank. Take it and run.

Chapter 9

Put Your Money into a Hedge Fund

D o you know what a hedge fund is? It is a pool of money guided by a great super genius to make stupendous profits for those fortunate enough to invest in it.

These entities were originally called hedge funds because they did not just make money if the stock market rose. No. They were arranged to "hedge" their investors' bets by selling short (of which much more to come), by dispersing investments in all sorts of different instruments beyond stocks (more to come on this, too), and by other brilliant devices.

These came into great prominence in the 1960s on Wall Street when Wall Street "hit a wall," so to speak and money just going long was hard to get. Some hedge fund managers made immense profits—for a while—by buying into early stock offerings that were not open to purchase by ordinary investors. When the companies offering these insiders cheap, early stock went public and the stock price soared, as it occasionally did, immense profits were made by the hedge funds.

The hedge fund managers also thought of other innovations, especially in how they billed. Because they were able to convince investors that they, the hedge fund managers, had both special expertise and special insider connections that were guaranteed to make money beyond what ordinary brokers or mutual funds could make, the hedge fund managers were able to charge exceptionally high, some might say, astonishing fees.

A normal index fund today might put you into an index for less than two-tenths of 1 percent and not charge more than pennies to maintain the account, and no fee or almost none to sell the stocks in the fund. A normal, nondiscount broker back in the 1960s might have charged 1 or 2 percent at most to make a trade, then pennies to maintain the account. But the hedge fund manager of the 1960s would charge something like 2 percent of the assets in the account each year—and then a staggering 20–30 percent of the profits beyond the rate on Treasury bonds.

Years ago, as I like to repeat, one of the smartest lawyers I ever knew told me that while he might not know much about trying a case, he had learned how to bill. That turned out to be mainly what the hedge fund managers knew. It turned out that few if any of them were great geniuses for the ages.

Much of the bloom came off the hedge fund rose in the late 1960s and early 1970s when the market was whacked by world events, especially worldwide inflation and dramatic spikes in interest rates. More of the bloom came off when the early buying of cheap stock turned out to have been of questionable legality and the later rise in price of the same company's stock allegedly might have been manipulated.

The great geniuses took their money and went off to play in much the same way Bernie Kornfeld had gone to play (before he went to prison).

Hedge funds in any numbers disappeared until the 1990s or so, and they reappeared like locusts during the first Internet bubble. They somehow managed to get in early in offerings of Internet dot-coms that soared into the stratosphere and paid off fantastically to investors. Then they soared even more when the managers turned out to be great geniuses at predicting the movements of stocks and bonds and currencies.

All of these accomplishments were touted wildly by the media, who treated the managers of hedge funds that had been successful for six months or a year as if they were the Magi come to lay gifts at the feet of the Saviour. The hedge fund managers' homes were written up. Their art and yachts were written up. Their wives' clothing designers were written up. And there was just the hint, the slightest hint, that there might be an opening for you, ordinary millionaire from Tulsa or Tulare, to get onto the gravy train to super wealth. You just had to drop off your millions and agree to pay that "2 and 20" and you were all set.

Then this whole structure was kicked into hyper-space when a few hedge fund managers were found to have correctly predicted the crash in real estate and to have made billions for themselves and their investors by their brilliance. The ordinary well-to-do begged to get in.

The kindly souls of Wall Street were there to help. They created "funds of funds" (back to the pioneer Bernie Kornfeld again) and encouraged investments by the peons. Only the peons had to pay 3 percent each year on the invested funds plus 30 percent on gains above the hurdle rate, which is generally the rate on so-called risk-free Treasury bonds.

But who cares if you are paying 30 percent on gains of 100 percent while the overall market is sinking or treading water? Find the hedge fund warehouse and back up the truck!

Meanwhile, pretty much anyone with fairly rudi-mentary training and certification could become a hedge fund manager. You didn't need to have a joint math and physics PhD from Cal Tech to call yourself a hedge fund manager. You basically just had to, well, call yourself a hedge fund manager and rake in the cash. Only as of very recently would you have to be a certified financial planner.

And the big investment banks would help you raise money and also give you office space, and all you had to do was arrange to do your trades through them. It was all really great. As Pink Floyd so aptly sang, "And did we tell you the name of the game, boy. We call it Riding the Gravy Train."

Now this just goes to show how cruel life is. It turned out that upon closer inspection, and upon actually looking at the numbers for the performance of the hedge funds that reported their performance, and after deducting all those fees, hedge funds barely outperformed index funds at all. In general, in good years for the stock market, the indexes outperformed the average hedge funds. That was true even in some of the not so good years.

And the hedge funds that didn't report? Well, we don't know about them. They might be discreet and they might be dead. If they died, taking much of their investors' money with them, they generally would be dropped from the calculation of hedge fund returns. They would not be counted as a zero in the numerator and a one in the denominator, which would make them drag down the returns of hedge funds generally.

No, they would simply be dropped from the calculation, which makes the hedge funds look a LOT better.

Long years ago, a woman at an investing conference said to me, "Ben, there are no free lunches in the bond market." She was right. She might have added that there are no free lunches in any market. There are no free lunches anywhere you invest.

She might have also added that there's a sucker born every minute and two to take him—and that many of these who are born to take him call themselves hedge fund managers.

But the beauty part of all of this is that none of it applies to you!

There are a few hedge fund managers who make money year upon year in outlandish amounts. You will be one of the fortunate few who choose those dudes to manage your money. You will be one of those who picks the winners and then, just as those guys' hands get a bit cold, you will switch to the ones with the hot hands.

Statistics and history and probability mean nothing to you. You have magic coming out of your fingertips. You are a magic man or woman and you will choose the right guys and gals at the right hedge funds.

Of course, for the ordinary investor, it would be tricky to do this. For example, John Paulson, a legendary hedge fund trader, made billions for himself and his investors betting against the housing bubble. Then, within months, his investments began to underperform the market as the huge indexes swung to major gains. Many of his investors headed for the exits.

Is this likely to happen to you? Again, no. Why? Because you're you. How many times do I have to tell you? You are an amazing man or woman, an Ubermensch—and history means nothing to you. Nothing at all.

Chapter 10

Try Strategies That No One Else Has Ever Thought of . . . You Can Out-Think the Market

The basic John Q. Public—type might look for a time to invest when the ratio of price to earnings is low compared with trends over long historical periods. The average Janette investor might search for stocks (indexes of stocks) when the ratio of the price-to-book value of the companies in the index is low. Or, as Phil DeMuth and I (mostly Phil) have pointed out, that ordinary investor might look for times to invest when the prices of stocks are just plain lower than they have been over long recent periods.

It has been shown beyond a doubt that these are good metrics for selecting stock indexes.

Persons who buy at these times tend to make more money than persons who just buy in whenever they feel like it.

Or, the average investor might look for stocks in countries that have just gone through some natural disaster—such as the 2011 earthquake and tsunami in Japan—and note if the index of the main companies in that nation has taken a sudden fall of good size. The investor might think, "It is NOT different this time. The Japanese are an incredibly industrious people. They will rebound after this tragedy. Even with a long recession dragging them down, they will rally to at least the levels prior to the natural disaster.

Betting that there will be a reversion to the mean after a drastic deviation from the mean is usually a fine bet.

But that is way too simple for you. No, you should try to find some fundamental flaw in the way the entire stock market is priced and the way stocks generally are sold or bought. You should find that planetary conjunctions are really what make the market move. Or that dates on the calendar are of great importance in determining what makes stocks move. For example, you might find that selling in certain months will make money for you even if there is no reason that anyone can establish for such a belief.

Go for it. Try something that no one else has tried. Make up your own rules. Make money as you always have—through the feelings in your fingertips when you make that trade.

Chapter 11

Use the Strategies That University Endowments and the Giant Players Use

Yes, again, old fuddy-duddies like Bogle and Buffett have told you that you should stick to the simple stuff and just buy broad indexes, especially when the prices are low by historical metrics, and hold onto them as long as you can. Yes, that has proved to be a fairly decent strategy.

But is it good enough for Yale? Is it good enough for Harvard? Is it good enough for the many billionaire families in this world? No. That means it's not good enough for you, bro.

How do the Ivies and Stanford endowments and the Rockefellers invest? They don't just go to Vanguard or Fidelity and buy the indexes. That is for sure. They don't just go to Merrill Lynch and buy an ETF of all Taiwanese stocks above a certain size.

No. They have far more sophisticated strategies. They buy immense plots of forestland and wait for the value of the land to rise as forest resources and property gets more valuable. Land! After all, they're not making any more of it. In fact, with global warming raising the level of the oceans and swamping some low-lying areas, land is becoming ever scarcer. Scarcity means an increase in price.

Plus, everyone wants wood. You can build homes with it. You can build boats with it. You can lay railroad ties with it or put up telephone poles. So that's why you should own forests. Forests. It is almost too basic. That's what you should do. Go buy a few acres of forestland near your home, sit on it, and forget it.

Yes, it's true that in recent years as the housing collapse has taken hold in the United States, many fewer homes are being built. That generally means less wood is being used. And, yes, as fewer homes are being built, there is less demand for forest products generally. But that's only temporary. That will only last a decade or so. In the meantime, you should own forestland.

How does the Gates Foundation invest? They sure as hell don't just go down to their broker and buy GM. They don't buy a share of Apple (although I am sure they wish they had bought a lot of those shares in late 2008). They sign up with private-equity firms that use immense amounts of leverage to buy whole companies, rip, strip, and flip them, or else just patiently rebuild them.

For example, they might buy the Ben Stein Corporation. Then they issue bonds and pay themselves a huge special dividend with the proceeds. Then they lay off some workers to build up cash flow so they can pay the interest on the bonds for a while. It might even work, and with really great management the company might flourish.

If they buy a company with 10 percent down and it goes up in value by 5 times, they have made something on the order of 50 times their money (minus commissions and slices for the agents but not adding in special dividends).

That sounds about right. You can do the same thing. Find a beaten-down small bakery or convenience store or motel in your town. Buy it mostly with borrowed money. Put your whole heart and soul into fixing it up, making it shine . . . and then try selling it.

Of course you may have to take some time out of your day job and your time with your family to make this work, but so what? We are talking about making some real serious money here.

Once you have that motel shining, go to the bank and refinance it to as high a level as you can. Use that money to party hearty. Then try to make the motel so profitable that you can pay off the loan. If it doesn't work, too bad for the bank. The folks there will take it like sports and just pat you on the back and wish you better luck next time.

Better yet, mortgage your home to the hilt, and use that as the down payment to buy several small motels.

Fix them up. Put color TVs and microwaves in every room. Spray the beds with insecticide to keep down the bedbugs. Then, when they get to be profitable, borrow more against them and buy some more motels and build them up, and soon you are a living, breathing Conrad Hilton.

Sell them and start thinking about what kind of jet you want. Don't worry at all about the possibility that you won't be able to sell them at a profit or even at break-even, and your loan will be called and you'll lose your house. That is not what happens to success stories like you. You will sell them for a huge gain and bask in your glory.

That is how the big boys play the game, and you want to wear the big-boy pants, don't you?

The big guys also take down huge positions in whole good-sized companies and then go to the board of directors of those companies and demand big changes or else they will vote against management and make management's life miserable.

Often, management will pay these raiders off or else have a special dividend to make the billionaire raiders go away.

That's what you should do, too. You should find a local bank, let's say, and buy some stock in it. Then go down to the office of the bank and demand changes to make the bank more successful.

Look, I know what you're thinking. You are thinking, "Well, that all sounds great, but I have a job and a family. I don't really have time to do all of those things and I don't really know much about real estate or private equity."

Fine. That's your problem. But I did tell you how to make it all happen, didn't I? If you don't want to pay attention, if you're too stuck in your little cautious world, then don't come crying to me when Yale's endowment is up 20 or 30 percent in a year.

Maybe you're just not cool enough for some of these strategies. Don't feel bad. It happens to lots of guys.

Chapter 12

Commodities Are Calling . . . Will You Answer the Phone?

Everything That Happens in Your Life Involves Commodities

E very kind of food is a commodity except for maybe water and that day is coming, too. There are food commodities for every single thing you eat, including vegetables and tacos. You can invest or speculate in any and all of them.

That car you drive is made of steel and glass and has rubber tires. There are commodities that go into every part of your car and also into the machines that make the parts for the cars. You can buy any or all of them.

You are probably sitting in a chair or flying on an airplane sitting in a seat as you read this. The fabric of the chair is made of chemicals that can be bought. The airplane is powered by petroleum products you can speculate on.

When you go to sleep tonight you might lie on a bed with steel springs (commodity), a cotton top (commodity) and lie under an electric blanket powered by coal (commodity). Your home may be cooled or heated by natural gas—that's a commodity, too.

The whole world is made up of things, and each thing is made of chemicals and each of these chemicals is a commodity or part of a commodity (there may be a few exceptions) that you can buy and speculate upon.

In the last several years (I am writing this in Summer of 2012) many commodities have risen spectacularly in price.

If you owned commodities and the price went up, you would make money. That is, for sure, the way that the power players do it.

How do you, a mere mortal, buy commodities? There are many different ways, but the surest, simplest way is to have your broker buy you a contract that allows you to buy a certain amount of a commodity— let's say oil of a certain grade—at a certain price for a certain period of time. That is, you might pay X dollars for the right to have a certain amount, say (just for laughs) 1,000 barrels of oil from the Cushing, Oklahoma, warehouse, of the grade called West Texas Intermediate Crude, delivered to you at $140 a barrel any time until June 30, 2012.

If oil is currently way below $140 a barrel, which it is right now, you would not have to pay a lot for that contract option.

But if some horrible war breaks out in the Persian Gulf and oil shipments are interrupted, you might see the price of oil skyrocket, maybe higher than $140 a barrel.

Then your contract is "in the money" and you start making real dough. Even if the price gets very close to $140 a barrel and you still have some time left on your option, you will make money. You could be rich if you bought a lot of options that were way out of the money and then suddenly found they were in the money or close to it.

The super beauty of this is something called *margin*.

Margin is really just another word for a loan. The brokerage lends you money to buy something—usually stocks, but also commodities—and the security for the loan is the stock or the commodity. You pay interest on the loan. It is like a mortgage on your stocks, and who ever heard of anyone having trouble with a mortgage? You get your loan and you buy something—a house, a condo, a stock—and watch its price rocket upward. (It's taking candy from a baby.)

I don't wish to complicate this but the beauty of this is obvious, is it not?

If you could buy only $10,000 worth of contracts on oil, let us say, and by some lucky fluke you qualify for margin, you can (just as an example) buy $20,000 worth of oil with your $10,000. Your broker will lend you the other $10,000 on the security of the contracts.

When and if oil rockets upward, you make double what you would have made if you had not gone on margin. You make the profit on the cash portion of the speculation AND you make the profit on the margin part.

And you wonder how people get rich.

Now you know. You make money with other people's money. That's how it's done, pal.

There is a little bit of a problem here though, and let's not sugar-coat it. Commodities can go down as well as up. Yes, even with China's voracious need for commodities of every kind, commodities can go down, too. They can go down a lot.

Even if you have read the most recent commodities newsletters, even if you watch CNBC faithfully, even if you read the *Wall Street Journal* cover to cover six days a week, you can still make a wrong bet on commodities.

If China's growth slows (as it apparently has lately), if there are immense finds of shale natural gas in the United States, if the president decrees that automobiles must be smaller and lighter, then the prices of corn, of hogs, of oil, of natural gas, of iron, of steel, of gasoline can fall. The falls may be temporary or they may be long lasting. But they can wipe out your gains and create losses very quickly.

If you are holding commodities on margin, the broker who loaned you the margin will call you and ask for more money so that the ratio of cash and commodities to the loan remains adequate. The term for this is "margin call," and if you get one out of the blue when your commodity is "limit down," you may find it upsetting. Especially if you get the call very early in the morning.

("Limit down" means the commodity has gone down as much as it is allowed to go down in one day. There are limits on how much a commodity can fluctuate per day to prevent wholesale collapses in price. Your humble servant has gotten a margin call. It can change your day a lot.)

So, going into commodities is risky. But going into commodities when you use borrowed money, or margin . . . that's a whole new ball game.

But isn't that what you wanted? Weren't you tired of living the same old humdrum boring life you have been living? Didn't you want some adventure?

Commodities, especially commodities in margin, can give you just the thrill you wanted.

Chapter 13

Go on Margin for Everything

While we're at it, why stop at margin for commodities? Why not go on margin for everything you buy in the way of investments? That greatly adds to your chances to make money on those stocks you are so great at picking.

If you buy 100 shares of a new, inventively named social media site for $15 each and the price goes up to $25, you make a measly $1,000. But if you buy 150 shares by borrowing against those shares and using margin, you are far, far ahead of the game. You might not have to put up any more cash (that would depend upon the margin requirements at the moment). And then if it goes up to $25, you make $1500.

Just think if you buy 15,000 shares on margin! Then, when it goes up, you are really rockin' and rollin.'

Of course, if it goes down such that your securities are inadequate collateral, you will be asked for immediate cash—or else you will be brusquely informed that you have been "sold out" of your position. That means your whole position is sold out so the broker can seize enough cash to pay off the loan. If the stock has gone down a lot, and you get sold out but the proceeds of the sale are not enough to cover the loan, you owe the difference as a personal debt of honor.

It has to be paid. There is no way around it. It isn't like a mortgage, where the lender's only recourse is (usually) to seize the house securing the loan. No, no, no.

In a forced margin sale, you are liable for every single penny you borrowed whether your stock sale covers the debt or not.

It works like this: say you buy 1,500 shares of that new social media site at $10, and the margin rule allows for a 33 percent margin. That means you put up $5,000 in cash and then can borrow $10,000 from your broker to complete the deal. The loan is secured 100 percent by your stock as long as the price stays at $15.

Then, let us say, the unthinkable happens and your stock in that new social media company falls to $3 per share. That means your total holdings are now worth only $4,500. But your debt has not changed. That's fixed. So you have to put up margin to keep the loan secured. That means you have to come up with $5,500 cash, pronto.

There now. Doesn't that make the stodgy old business of investing sound a LOT more interesting? That's especially true if your margin can be, say, 80 percent and you can really borrow a lot and you have to come up with a lot of cash in a great hurry if your stock collapses. Imagine the lively times you'll have!

Chapter 14

Sell Short

One of the great glories of our stock, commodities, and certain other markets is being able to make money by wagering that a stock or a commodity (or something else too exotic to think of right now) will go down. Yes, you can make money by selling short a stock or virtually anything else.

Here, in a simplified way, is how it works.

You go to your broker. You tell her you want to sell your stock in that new social media site short because you have a feeling in your fingertips that it's going down.

So, let's say you want to sell 1,000 shares short when the stock is trading at $15 per share. The broker "borrows" 1,000 shares of the stock from my account or someone else's account and sells it at $15, for a total proceeds of $15,000 (less fees).

That $15,000 appears as both a credit and a liability on your books. Yes, you have the $15,000. But you also have the legal obligation to repay the 1,000 shares to the other client's account within a set time. In the meantime, you pay interest to the broker for the borrowing of the stock.

Suppose your brilliant intuition about the stock is correct and it goes down to $5 per share. You then tell your broker to buy 1,000 shares for you. You buy the shares for a total of $5,000. You return the shares to their original owner (who probably had no idea they were gone in the first place). You have a profit of $10,000—the $15,000 you originally got for selling the stock you borrowed less the $5,000 you paid to replace it. Pretty nice day's work.

There are all kinds of fun variations on this theme. You can buy a "put" option, which allows you to sell the stock back to the brokerage for $15 per share, no matter what you paid for it, at any time during a long or short duration. That also allows you to profit from a downturn in the stock since you might be able to buy it at lower than the "put" price and make money on the difference.

You can buy an option on a put, which is self-explanatory, but also allows you to make money if the stock goes down. The beauty of a put (or an option on a put) is that it limits your risk, but we will get to that in a moment.

In fact, short sales, puts, options on puts, and similar but far more complex entities are used by the big boys on the Street to hedge their bets. If they make huge long buys on a security of an ETF or an index, they might also do some short selling or put buying or options on put buying to offset their losses if the stocks go in the wrong direction.

I know this sounds too good to be true, but there is just one big problem, one spectacularly great way to help ruin your portfolio. You can lose money on a short sale. In fact, on a true short sale, your possibilities of losing money are limitless. (Again, that's the appeal of the option.)

On the buy of a stock or commodity or bond, your loss is limited to the amount you have paid for that stock, commodity, or bond. You cannot lose more than you paid for it. Even if it goes to zero, you cannot lose more than you paid.

But with a short sale, you can lose a vast amount beyond what you paid. You can lose the entire difference between what you borrowed the stock for and the price you have to pay to replace it.

Just for example, suppose you believe that the new social media stock is priced at $15 but is going to $5. You sell short 10,000 shares. If your hunch is right and the stock goes down to $5, you have made 10,000 × $10, or 100,000 smackers. But suppose you go away on vacation and while you are gone, the stock corporation comes up with a new gizmo that allows you to plug it into your brain and become as smart as Al Gore. Then the stock goes to $100.

You hear on CNBC that the next move for this company is an app that allows you to plug it into your brain and lose weight. You hear the stock is headed for $200. Naturally, you want out. So you have to cover your short. You have to go into the market and buy

10,000 shares at $100 to cover your short position, lest you lose even more on your short. That costs you a cool million. Now, to be fair, you also got paid $15,000 when you sold short. But still, your loss is $985,000. That hurts.

Now let's be fair again. Rarely does a stock shoot up from $15 to $100 in a short time. But the example illustrates the problem. Your loss is measured by how far above the sale price you have to buy in. There is literally no limit on how high a stock or a commodity can go. There is no limit on how big your loss can be.

Out of such a problem are sleepless nights and forced sales of your residence made.

But, you will say, you just told me that the big boys on the Street use short sales. How come they do it if it's so dangerous?

BECAUSE THEY ARE THE BIG BOYS. Usually, they are playing with other people's money. Usually they hedge even the hedges. They have split-second alert systems and can sell very fast. They don't go on vacations when they have open positions.

I have a super-smart friend named Jim Rogers. He can and does sell short. He makes money at it. I would not dream of it. Why? Because he's big enough, tough enough, experienced enough, and quick enough to do it right. I'm not.

Neither are you.

But don't let that stop you.

Just as I told you that you could ruin your portfolio by trying the devices the big guys use in buying forestland, going into private equity, and greenmailing corporations, so you might as well try the big-boy play of selling short. Hey, it's only money.

Chapter 15

Do Not Have a Plan for Your Investing or for Your Financial Life Generally

U sually, the plan for most Americans is simple: seek to amass sufficient assets to meet your liabilities.

For most Americans, their number-one liability is providing enough jewelry for their daughter-in-law.

HA! Fooled you. You were not expecting that, were you?

No, seriously, as my dear pal, Ray Lucia, likes to tell me, a grown up's main financial plan has to be to match his or her assets with the liability of providing for himself/herself and his or her adult family after he or she stops working.

A secondary asset/liability issue might be paying for a child's college education. In today's sad educational climate, it might also be necessary to pay for a child's entire schooling at a very expensive private school, starting in elementary school.

Match assets and liabilities. That sounds fairly basic, doesn't it? All you have to know to do it is the rate of return on your investments and how much it will cost you to live after you retire. That means knowing how long you are going to live and in what state of health and (this is a killer) what the rate of inflation will be.

This is actually incredibly, unbelievably complex. You can at best come up with prior decades' rate of return on stocks and bonds and real estate. You cannot POSSIBLY know what the future rate of return will be. Likewise, you cannot possibly know what the inflation rate will be after you retire or even before you retire.

You can do approximations and usually these will work fairly well. There are things called Monte Carlo simulations that my pal Phil DeMuth likes to work with. They play out all possibly scenarios to give you a taste of what you might face in the future—based, of course, on what happened in the past.

But to know with precision how much you are going to need and how much you will have available to you . . . that is an incredibly difficult undertaking. No, not just difficult: impossible.

You could try to simplify it by living with such extreme frugality that your needs will be small compared with your assets no matter what happens. That was my parents' solution and it worked beautifully for them. Even after they were well-to-do people in their 80s in the decade of the 1990s, they lived as if they were graduate students at The University of Chicago in 1937. They simply never were extravagant about anything. Thus, they never had to worry about lacking large amounts of money—even though they were extremely careful about spending small amounts of money. They literally had money to burn, but they never burned it.

But was it fun? Did they live the life of a James Bond or a Hugh Hefner? No, they lived a very quiet life. They claim they were happy, but were they? Can anyone be happy who is sensible? Question asked and question answered. By the way, even though they never burned the money when they were alive, it turned out that they made a catastrophic mistake by not doing anything particularly clever about their estate planning. The IRS got to burn most of their money (which should have gone to my sister and me).

Another plan . . . you can go with an inflation-indexed annuity. These little beauties pay you a set amount at the commencement of their term, and then increase the payments as inflation mounts. Sounds great, doesn't it? It is, but there is a problem. They are a bit expensive to buy. They can cost up to a few percent of your assets per year, although usually less.

Now, some smart guy will say, "Of course they're expensive to buy. They offer a lifesaving product. How much would you pay to save your life?"

But, another voice whispers in your ear . . . it's all so darned complicated and so expensive and requires so much thought and discipline . . . why do it at all?

Because remember, to follow a plan, most of us have to severely discipline spending (but not if we are NBA forwards). And we have to really throw ourselves into saving. Do we really want to spoil the good times with that kind of discipline?

Do we really want to deny ourselves the thrill of obeying the impulse to spend, to buy, to live on the edge?

Tell the truth now: Don't you feel better when you spend than when you save? For some deep psychological reason, men and women just plain feel good about spending. There is nothing anywhere near as pleasant for most of us about saving.

Yes, when the bill comes, that's not so great. But up until then, isn't it really a lot more fun to spend than to save?

Just let your feelings wash over you and float you out to sea on a soothing Caribbean current of money bliss. Forget about a plan. Anyway, haven't you ever heard the saying, "Man makes plans and God laughs"?

It happens to be true. So, instead of making plans that might not come true, just don't make a plan at all and see where you come out. You might like it, or you might not like it. You'll just have to see.

Chapter 16

Do It All Yourself

Y ou don't need advisers or experts. You can do it all with your own brilliant intuition. You don't need a guiding hand or a restraining arm. You just do what you feel is best. You don't need to hire anyone with experience or knowledge. You were born knowing all you need to know, and now you are a grown-up and you can do it without some broker or financial planner as a surrogate parent. You left that parent thing behind long ago. So just go for it, and do it all by yourself. Experience and knowledge mean nothing where money is concerned.

Chapter 17

Pay No Attention at All to Taxes

What to do about taxes is another one of those quibbles that eats up your time and money. Why bother with it? Don't worry about whether some investments, like index funds, belong in tax-favored accounts like IRAs. Don't worry about whether others, like cash or super-low-yield bonds, belong in non-tax-favored accounts. And when it comes to your estate plans? Don't worry about whether you have done anything to protect posterity. After all, what has posterity ever done for you?

Taxes only amount to about half of your estate, and you'll be dead anyway. So, who cares?

And taxes on capital gains—at 15 percent as I write this, but possibly to go up a lot and soon—they are an important source of income for our federal government. Don't try to cheat Uncle Sam out of money he needs.

Don't have a tax planner or adviser. Just let the chips fall where they may.

Chapter 18

Believe That Those People You See on TV Can Actually Tell the Future

I know you harbor a secret belief that no one, absolutely no one, can tell the future. But that's wrong. If a man or woman is on a TV show about the economy, he or she can tell the future. Likewise, if a man or woman has a column about money anywhere in any format, he or she can tell the future.

It doesn't matter if he's been wrong over and over in the past. This time, he or she will be right about the future.

Yes, it is true that even billionaire geniuses like Warren Buffett often get things wrong. Even Presidents and Supreme Court Justices get things wrong. Your humble scribe very often gets things wrong. (Or at least I have in the past. I never will in the future.)

But as of today, you can believe every prediction from every expert you see or read about.

Likewise, every mutual fund manager and hedge fund guru can tell the future.

Somewhere in the husk of your brain, there might be a spark that glows and says, "Hey, if anyone can really tell the future, he'll be the richest man in the world in about a week . . . and these guys aren't."

Never mind that. From now on, there will be people who can tell the future, and you can find them with ease on TV. Trust them. Follow them wherever they lead. Pay no attention at all to what their own track record is with their investments. Just follow them blindly, for they can see into the future and they can see around corners—and you cannot.

They have miraculous powers no one else has. Why else would they be on TV or have newsletters or blogs? They and they alone can take the uncertainty out of life.

Chapter 19

Do Not Start Even Thinking about Any of This until the Absolutely Last Moment

T hat is, don't even start to think about planning for retirement until retirement is almost upon you. Don't plan ahead. Do not start laying money aside when you are young. Yes, it's true that if you start at age 21 putting away money regularly year by year, month by month, by the time you are 65, if you get any interest or capital gain at all, you will be sitting pretty at that retirement party. Think about it: Put up $1,000 a year from age 21 to age 65, and if you can earn 8 percent a year, you will have $327,000 at the end of that time. If you put up $10,000 a year, you will have $3,270,000.

On the other hand, if you spend that money, you can have a lot of fun. You can buy a great car, go on trips to Nassau, buy nice clothes, go on dates, and buy drinks all around at your local bar. You can seem to be—and be—a big wheel and a rich guy even though you are really digging yourself into a deep hole.

But you will have those shining moments when all eyes at the bar are on you, and they are big, admiring eyes, big admiring blue eyes. And isn't that worth a lot more than having money sitting around in a worthless retirement account not doing anything but laughing at you from the printed page?

So maybe, when you are 60 or 61, start putting money aside for your retirement, but not a moment before. How will you get the amount of money you need? Who cares? You are a free spirit, not an accountant.

Chapter 20

Don't Believe That Any of This Matters Very Much, This Money Stuff

A fter all, life is in session. Life is about beauty and adventure, about finding the right swashbuckling yachting captain with wavy blonde hair and bright blue eyes who will come along and sweep you off your feet.

Life is about losing the man you thought was yours forever (he committed suicide because he said you were so boring he would rather be dead that spend another moment with you), and then finding redemption by moving to a South Pacific island and starting a vegetable garden and a cooking school. You'll teach the natives how to cook broccoli, something they never even knew existed. You can do all of this in a grass shack. Money doesn't mean a thing to you. Instead of money you will have all of that broccoli and the admiration of the islanders. So, even if you make every mistake in the book about money, you will still have that broccoli and that cooking school . . . and the golden-haired yacht captain whom destiny is bringing toward you.

Really, again, how big a deal is money when you are in an island chain in the middle of the ocean? And that can be your life any old time. So don't even think about the whole subject of your portfolio and how it's doing or about how your money is doing at all. You can always be a beachcomber. You can always go live on your family's estates in the Cotswolds. Your retirement? Does a broccoli grower need to think about retirement? Does a landed English country gentleman?

What about paying for your kids' education? Well, here, let me borrow, as I so often do, from the Gipper, Mr. Ronald Reagan himself. When asked how he felt about the fact that his tax cuts were creating immense budget deficits, and how he felt about the likelihood that these would be a burden on posterity, Mr. Reagan aptly asked, "What has posterity ever done for me?"

Or, look at it in biblical terms. When Jesus Christ was asked how the poor might provide clothes for themselves, he replied, "Behold the lilies of the field. They toil not. Neither do they spin. Yet Solomon in all his glory was not so arrayed. . . . Therefore take no thought for the morrow." (I am paraphrasing here.)

The whole subject of money is nothing compared with lilies of the field or broccoli. So just forget about all of it and inhale deeply.

Chapters 21—49

How to Ruin Your Greatest Asset—You

Now we are going to switch gears.

For most of us, our single largest earning assets are ourselves. Most of us will never have enough money in interest, or in the stock market, or in real estate to pay our bills until we retire—if then. BUT!!! You are yourself a huge earning asset—your brains, your charm, your elegance, your strong back. These can and will protect you and pay your bills.

So, again, you are the key part of your portfolio. Here is a brief summary of how to ruin that asset. I am making it really brief.

Chapter 21
Choose a Career with No Possibility of Advancement

Choose a career where your starting pay and your ending pay are likely to be the same. Choose a career where your work makes no difference to people's lives or where that difference cannot be measured. That guarantees a low wage.

Chapter 22
Choose a Career with Little Chance for a Good Income

That could sometimes mean manual labor and sometimes not. It might mean anything at all in the world of art or music. It often means a career where the top dogs make billions—like Mick Jagger or Axl Rose—and the ordinary guy or gal has to supplement his or her income waiting tables. Don't choose a career like law where, once you get on the track, your income rises steadily.

Chapter 23
Choose Lots of Education over Lots of Pay

Make sure you have that PhD in origami design even if it adds not one penny to your bottom line. See the note about the lilies of the field in Chapter 20.

Chapter 24
Show No Respect for Your Boss or Fellow Workers

People like to be treated like dirt. They respect you more for it. So show utter contempt for the people who supervise you and who work with you. That will show them who the real boss is—YOU, YOU, YOU!

Chapter 25
Don't Learn Much about Your Job, Industry, or Employers . . . Just Wing It

Don't be a grind or a bookworm. If you can't pick it up just by your first impressions of it, don't bother with it. Nothing is worth spending a lot of time reading or learning.

Chapter 26
Do the Minimum Just to Get By

Don't be a showoff. Don't be an ass-kisser. Don't be a Goody Two-Shoes.

Chapter 27
Show Up in Torn Jeans, Unshaven, Unwashed, Any Old Way You Feel Like Showing Up

You are not a cog in a machine. You are not in the military. You are a free man or woman.

Chapter 28
Show No Regard for the Truth

The absolute truth means something to mathematicians, one supposes, but not to poets and artists and visionaries like you. Did Keats care about the truth? Did van Gogh? Did Bernie Madoff? What they created was their truth, and as the saying goes, "We all have truths. Mine do not have to be the same as yours."

Chapter 29
Display Open Contempt for Your Job, Your Fellow Workers, Your Boss, and Your Clients/Customers

You are Marlon Brando. You are Arnold Schwarzenegger. You are above the law. It is that simple. The others are worker bees. You are the Queen Bee.

Chapter 30
Act Like You Are Morally Superior to Your Job and Your Colleagues

Act as if your colleagues and bosses were all organized-crime figures or con men and cheats. You are morally better than they are and don't hesitate to let them know it. Their business or government duties are basically theft and fraud. You are a knight in shining armor. It isn't complicated.

Chapter 31
Do Not Be Punctual

That is for servants and lackeys, which you definitely are not. 'Nuff said.

Chapter 32
Don't Hesitate to Have a Cocktail or Two at Lunch

Your workday is stressful. Who is to judge you if you decide you need to unwind a bit at lunch with your friends and colleagues? You can hold it and you'll be better for it—and if you're not better for it—too darned bad.

Chapter 33
Gossip and Sow Divisiveness at Work

Make sure you set staff members against each other. Make sure you have people at work fighting with each other instead of getting anything useful done. Don't worry: The word will soon get back to the powers that be about who is responsible.

Chapter 34
Second-Guess Everyone around You at Work, Especially Your Boss

People in charge like to have their subordinates question their decisions, so do it early and often.

Chapter 35
Threaten Your Boss and Employer with Litigation

You know your rights. You are not going to get pushed around. Just let the whole workplace know that one wrong look, and bang, it's sexual harassment. One wrong word, and it's disability discrimination. No matter what, you will find a way to sue and make your employers' lives miserable. They will respect you for asserting yourself. Besides, people like to be sued.

Chapter 36
Look for Grievances at Work

Don't forgive. Don't forget. Think the worst of everyone. Start each day believing that the other guy is going to screw you over. Next thing you know, you'll have it come true.

Chapter 37
Make Sexual Advances to Anyone You Find Attractive

You're a play-uhh, uh-huh. Let the whole world know it and right away—you'll be happier and they'll be happier. Women and men want to be noticed and flirted with, so be a Casanova or a cougar in the cubicle. Your colleagues will respect you more for it. And don't hesitate to tell dirty jokes to get someone "in the mood" when you're ready to play.

Chapter 38
Make Excessive Phone Calls, Texts, and E-Mails on Company Time

Again, you aren't a robot. You have to maintain your social connections. Play the high-tech social-life game as hard as you can. Everyone else is doing it. Why not you?

Chapter 39
Play Video Games at Work and Make Loud Noises as You Do

When you get bored with that, look for porn on the Internet, the more explicit the better. Definitely with the sound turned up. Who cares if people see you? This isn't George Orwell's *1984*. There is no Ministry of Truth, no Thought Police. You are allowed to do what you want, and you are not in prison when you are on the clock. If you need to see some manly or womanly action to take a break from your insanely hard work, hey, pal, you're allowed.

Chapter 40
Make and Keep Lots of Personal Appointments on Company Time

You have a life. You are entitled to live your life. If you don't get in your full quota of hours today, you will some other day.

Chapter 41
Listen to Your Colleagues' Conversations and Snoop on Their E-Mails

Then share what you learn with the other people in the office or the workshop.

Chapter 42
Talk about How Much Better Earlier Employers Were Than Your Current Employer

Bosses like to be told when they could do things better, and you telling them how they could do it better will help them be better people. They'll eventually thank you for it.

Chapter 43
Brag about Your Great Family Connections

Let everyone know that you have parents who can pull strings and get your boss in trouble, or get you promoted no matter how you act. Everyone at work needs to know of your superior work and social status so you get the proper respect.

Chapter 44
Pad Your Expense Account

No one will notice. Your cheapskate bosses don't pay you enough anyway. That little extra bit in your expense account is rightfully yours in any event. If anyone questions you about it, just tell him you'll cut him in if he keeps quiet.

Chapter 45
Borrow Money from Your Fellow Employees and Don't Pay It Back

They know that times are tight and you might need a bit to slide by. And who needs it more? You or they? And when you borrow it, don't pay it back. After all, how are you any better off if you pay it back? Answer: You're not. If you don't pay it back, you are money-good. So . . . you get the picture, right?

Chapter 46
Question, Mock, and Belittle Your Tasks

Chapter 47
Flirt with Your Colleagues' Significant Others

Let them know there's an alpha male or a cougar on the prowl. They'll pay attention.

Chapter 48
Proselytize at Work and Belittle Anyone Who Doesn't Share Your Political or Religious Beliefs

That will let everyone who needs to know who's in with the Man Upstairs and who isn't . . . and, again, will get you the status you deserve. Plus it will properly shame all the blasphemers and heretics who don't understand your divine connections.

Chapter 49
Say Anything You Want That Comes into Your Head

You should never feel any need for self-restraint. It is entirely up to you, what you say and believe. Never forget it.

■ ■ ■

And now, I have to take a nap.

About the Author

B en Stein is the son of noted economist and writer, Herbert Stein, and Mildred Stein, also an economist.

He studied economics at Columbia and also at Yale where he earned a law degree. He worked as an economist at The U.S. Department of Commerce, and as a writer about economics for The Bureau of National Affairs. He has been a trial lawyer, a speech writer for Presidents Nixon and Ford, a teacher of Law and Economics at Pepperdine, and a columnist for *The Wall Street Journal* and *The New York Times Sunday Business Section*.

He wrote extremely long analyses of financial misconduct and market anomalies for *Barron's* for many years. He has been an expert witness in many federal and state securities fraud cases. He has written over a dozen books on investing, including most recently many books on finance co-written with Phil DeMuth, many of which became *New York Times* best sellers.

He is a regular commentator on finance for Fox News and a frequent guest on CNN. He also has been a contributor to *CBS Sunday Morning* for some years. He speaks frequently to investor groups. He lives in Southern California with his wife of many years, Alexandra Denman.